ISBN: 9798341063433

Printed in the United States of America

WE ARE NOT THE ENEMY

How Pre-Millennial Generations Struggle to Understand Millennial and Later Generations

Billy J Riggs

TABLE OF CONTENTS

CHAPTER ONE
Across the Generational Divide

John "Pops" Harrison had been on the road for nearly four days now, driving his old Ford F-150 across the vastness of America with his grandson, Eric. The plan was simple: a cross-country trip from their home in Pennsylvania to California, stopping at a few national parks along the way. Pops loved these open roads, the sprawling landscapes, the freedom of the journey. For him, America was still a land of opportunity and endless possibilities—a sentiment he'd carried with him since his youth.

Eric, though, was different. At twenty-four, he was part of the so-called "Generation Y," a generation born into a world that felt, to him, like it was in decline. While Pops marveled at the towering mountains and wide blue skies, Eric spent most of the time staring out the window, lost in thought or on his phone, scrolling through the endless feed of news, social media, and complaints about how the world had gone wrong.

They had just passed through Kansas when Eric finally spoke up. "You ever think about how unfair everything is, Pops?" John glanced over, noting the frustration on his grandson's face. "What do you mean, kiddo?" "I mean, look at everything. Housing prices are ridiculous, college debt is crushing people, healthcare's a mess, and jobs barely pay enough to live. It's like the system was set up for you guys, and now we're just left to clean up the mess."

Pops didn't say anything at first. He let the words hang in the air as the hum of the road filled the silence. He'd heard similar sentiments before, but it never got any easier to hear. He wasn't blind to the struggles Eric's generation faced. But it puzzled him that people like his grandson seemed to think they were starting from scratch—as if his generation had handed them nothing but rubble.

"You think we had it easy, huh?" Pops finally asked, his voice steady but curious. Eric shrugged. "Well, yeah. I mean, your generation had stable jobs, pensions, affordable homes. You didn't have to worry about climate change or massive inequality like we do." Pops chuckled softly, though not unkindly. "Son, we didn't have everything handed to us either. We had our own struggles— wars, recessions, inflation. We fought for the things we have now. We built this country up after it was knocked down. But that's just life, you know? Each generation has its own battles."

"But you don't get it," Eric pressed. "It's different now. The whole system is broken. We're just... trying to survive in the wreckage." Pops scratched his chin, trying to piece together how things had become so polarized between their generations. He knew Eric wasn't lazy or ungrateful, but he couldn't wrap his head around why so many young people seemed to look at the past with such disdain.

To Pops, it felt like every achievement, every innovation, every ounce of sweat poured into building this country was being dismissed as a mistake. "Maybe it feels broken to you," Pops said after a long pause. "But you gotta understand, everything we did, we did because we believed in making life better for our kids and grandkids. We weren't perfect, sure. But we worked our tails off.

We didn't wake up one day and get handed houses and pensions. I was lucky to get a job at the factory after high school, and I worked there for thirty-five years. Do you think I loved every minute of it? Heck no. But it gave me the life I have now. It gave me the chance to take you on this trip."

Eric sighed. "I know you worked hard, Pops. But things are just different now. It feels like we're paying for mistakes we didn't make. Like the older generations had their shot and left us with nothing but problems to fix." Pops thought about that for a moment. He didn't deny that the world had its share of problems, but it stung to hear Eric talk as if the sacrifices made by his generation didn't count for much.

"You know," he said, "we didn't create all these problems on purpose. We did the best we could with what we had. And we thought we were leaving the world better than we found it." "But were you?" Eric asked, his voice softer now. "I mean, look at where we are. Climate disasters, political division, financial instability. It just feels like everything's coming apart at the seams."

Pops could hear the weight in Eric's words. It was a heavy burden, no doubt. "Maybe you're right," he conceded. "Maybe we didn't fix everything we should've. But that doesn't mean you can't. Every generation's gotta fight its own fight. We fought ours, and now it's your turn. The thing is, you gotta stop blaming us and start figuring out what you're gonna do about it."

Eric was quiet for a long while after that. The road stretched out endlessly before them, the sun dipping low in the sky, casting a golden hue over the plains. "I don't hate you guys," Eric finally said. "I just wish it didn't feel like everything's stacked against us."

Pops nodded. "I get it. I do. But you've got something going for you that we didn't—you've got more information, more technology, more tools at your disposal. You're more connected. You've got the power to change things in ways we never dreamed of."

Eric stared out the window again, but this time, Pops could tell he wasn't just lamenting the state of the world. He was thinking. Maybe, just maybe, the weight of responsibility was starting to shift from the past to the future.

As the sun dipped below the horizon, Pops turned on the headlights and kept driving, the road ahead uncertain but full of possibility. "Just remember, kid," Pops said quietly. "We didn't build this country for ourselves. We built it for you. Now it's your turn to take the wheel."

CHAPTER TWO

A Tale of Two Upbringings

The story of the typical American childhood has evolved dramatically over the past seventy years. From the Baby Boomers, who grew up in the post-World War II era, to the Millennials and Gen Y. The challenges faced by each generation were shaped by the socioeconomic climate, technological advancements, and cultural expectations surrounding work and adulthood. Although there are universal themes of childhood such as curiosity, growth, and the search for independence, the specifics of how each generation transitioned from childhood to adulthood reveal striking contrasts.

For Baby Boomers (1946–1964) childhood unfolded during an era of economic growth, particularly in the United States. The 1950s and 1960s saw a flourishing middle class, driven by the post-war industrial boom, suburbanization, and government policies such as the GI Bill, which provided education and housing opportunities for veterans. This environment set the stage for a relatively stable upbringing.

Baby Boomers were raised during a time when one income could often support an entire household. Many grew up in homes where their fathers worked stable, often unionized jobs, while their mothers stayed home to manage the household. However, not all Baby Boomers were part of this idyllic narrative. Many faced challenges of poverty, especially in rural areas or among minority communities, where systemic inequalities persisted. Still, the overall economic environment provided a sense of optimism that supported the idea that hard work and discipline would be rewarded with financial stability and upward mobility.

Technology during the Baby Boomers' childhood was mechanical and industrial, not digital. Most homes had radios and, by the mid-1950s, televisions. Cars and household appliances were becoming more accessible to the average family, offering convenience but not the kind of digital connectivity we associate with modern life.

Communication was face-to-face or by telephone, and news came via newspapers, TV, or radio. In the past, reporters focused primarily on delivering the facts, often adhering to the principle of "just the facts" journalism. Their role was to present unbiased information, allowing viewers or readers to form their own opinions about the news. This straightforward approach emphasized objectivity and factual reporting.

Entertainment was simpler too. Kids played outside, rode bikes, or participated in community sports. Childhood was often defined by freedom of movement and imagination, unencumbered by the structured schedules of later generations.

Many Baby Boomers began working as teenagers. It was not uncommon for them to hold summer jobs or part-time work after school by the time they were 14 or 15. Work was seen as a character-building experience, instilling a sense of responsibility and independence. Jobs ranged from mowing lawns to working in grocery stores, gas stations, or family businesses. For most, entering the workforce wasn't an economic necessity but rather a rite of passage. By 18, many were either heading off to college, supported by affordable tuition, or entering the workforce directly with confidence that they could establish stable, long-term careers.

For Baby Boomers, the path to adulthood was relatively straightforward. Many married in their early twenties, bought homes shortly thereafter, and began careers they often expected to stay in for decades. The idea of a career was tied to a sense of loyalty to one's employer, and jobs typically came with benefits like pensions that provided financial security in old age. The post-war American Dream was within reach, offering a relatively predictable trajectory into adulthood and beyond.

Millennials and later generations, though slightly different in terms of years, share few similarities in how they experienced early childhood and adolescence, particularly regarding the rapid societal changes that defined the late 20th and early 21st centuries.

By the time Millennials and later generations were growing up, the economic landscape had changed drastically. The 1980s and 1990s saw rising income inequality, stagnant wages, and the decline of manufacturing jobs that had supported Baby Boomer households.

Families increasingly relied on dual incomes, with both parents working full-time, which shifted the family dynamic. While many Millennials and Gen Yers grew up in comfortable, middle-class homes, economic pressures, like rising healthcare and education costs, made financial stability harder to achieve. This was especially pronounced for those growing up in single-parent households or under the shadow of the 2008 financial crisis, which left lasting scars on their economic outlook.

Unlike Baby Boomers, Millennials and Gen Yers were the first to experience the digital revolution during their formative years. Childhoods of the late 1980s and 1990s were defined by the advent of personal computers, the internet, and mobile phones. By the time they reached adolescence, social media had become ubiquitous, and access to information was at their fingertips.

This technology revolution reshaped everything from education to social interaction. Children were introduced to the concept of screen time, and their worlds expanded digitally in ways their grandparents could hardly have imagined.

Yet, this tech-infused childhood came with a cost. The rise of social media and constant connectivity also brought about new forms of pressure, cyberbullying, social comparison, and the pressure to be "always on." Where Baby Boomers had enjoyed privacy in their personal growth, Millennials and later generations have grown up in a world where their lives could be broadcast online.

Television news journalists assume a more interpretive role. Instead of just reporting facts, they analyze current events, providing their preferred context, background, and opinion on what the news might mean for viewers' lives. This shift is driven in part by the 24-hour news cycle, the rise of partisan media, and the demand for immediate analysis. As a result, journalism now frequently blends news reporting with commentary, aiming to control the broader narrative and implications of events in society, politics, and daily life.

For Millennials and Gen Y, entering the workforce has been one of the defining challenges of their adulthood. Many took on part-time jobs during high school, much like their grandparents.

However, the reasons were different. For many, working was not just a character-building exercise but a necessity to save for rising college costs or contribute to household expenses. The traditional after-school job at the mall or restaurant was supplemented by a growing "gig economy," with many Millennials turning to freelance work or side gigs before they even graduated.

After the financial crisis of 2008, the job market for young adults became increasingly unstable. While Boomers had been able to secure full-time employment with benefits directly after high school or college, many Millennials found themselves stuck in part-time or low-wage positions, often unrelated to their degrees. The promise of upward mobility that had defined the Baby Boomer generation felt elusive, replaced by uncertainty and a growing sense of precarity.

The markers of adulthood like marriage, homeownership, and starting a family were delayed for Millennials and Gen Y compared to Baby Boomers. Crushed by student debt, stagnant wages, and high housing costs, these generations entered adulthood in a far less stable economic climate. For many, living with parents into their twenties or even thirties became a necessity, not a choice. Marriage rates declined, and homeownership became increasingly out of reach for many young adults. While Baby Boomers had been able to buy homes in their twenties, Millennials often found themselves renting well into their thirties and forties.

The modern economy also reshaped the idea of a "career." Whereas Baby Boomers often stayed with one employer for decades, Millennials and Gen Yers were more likely to switch jobs frequently, driven by a lack of stability, better opportunities elsewhere, or disillusionment with corporate structures.

The childhood experiences of Baby Boomers versus Millennials and later generations reveal a profound shift in how socioeconomics, technology, and cultural expectations shape our journey to adulthood. Baby Boomers, coming of age in an era of prosperity and optimism, often found security in stable jobs, affordable homes, and clear paths to adulthood.

Later generations have created a more complex world, defined by economic volatility, rapid technological change, and shifting societal norms. While Boomers enjoyed the promise of the American Dream, their grandchildren grapple with a reality that feels more uncertain and precarious. So what happened between the Baby Boomer and Millennial generations?

CHAPTER THREE

The Turbulent Generations

By the time Generation Jones, Generation X, and the Xenials had reached adulthood, they had experienced their fair share of struggles. Born in the turbulent decades between the 1960s and early 1980s, these generations came of age during times of social upheaval, economic instability, and shifting family dynamics. They had watched their Baby Boomer parents navigate a rapidly changing world, often feeling lost in the cracks between idealism and harsh realities.

The Vietnam War, civil rights movements, recessions, and the rise of divorce rates shaped their formative years. Many of them grew up in homes where both parents worked, or in single-parent households, forced to mature quickly and take on responsibilities that felt burdensome.

For them, childhood was often marked by a sense of neglect, if not physically, then emotionally. Parents of previous generations were less likely to hover over every decision or coddle every failure.

These children often felt they had to fend for themselves. If they lost, they lost. If they failed, it was made clear without softening the blow. It was a world where resilience wasn't optional; it was required.

As Generation Jones, X, and Xenials grew up and started their own families, they wanted something different for their children. They looked back on their own experiences and decided that they wouldn't let their kids feel the same sting of isolation or failure they had known. In their minds, protecting their children from the harsh realities they had faced was an act of love.

What started with the best of intentions would gradually lead to the creation of an entirely new approach to parenting, one that ultimately set the stage for a generation ill-prepared for the world that awaited them.

The first shift came in how these generations viewed competition. To those who had grown up in the 1970s and 1980s, competition often felt like a zero-sum game. Only the winners received recognition, and everyone else went home empty-handed. Whether it was on the soccer field, in the classroom, or at school competitions, the idea was simple: you either succeeded or you didn't.

As parents, Generation Jones, X, and Xenials couldn't shake the memory of being overlooked when they were younger, the sting of not being "good enough" gnawed at them. They began to question the necessity of making children feel like failures at such a young age. Why should kids be judged so harshly for their efforts? Didn't simply trying deserve recognition?

Thus, the participation trophy was born. No longer would only the best and brightest walk away with something to show for their efforts. Now, everyone would receive a token of their involvement. This wasn't about celebrating mediocrity, they reasoned, but about fostering self-esteem. Every child who played in a game or took part in an activity would be told that their participation mattered. Whether they won or lost, they were special simply because they had shown up.

Parents believed this would encourage children to continue trying, to build their confidence without the weight of failure hanging over their heads. What they didn't anticipate was that it would inadvertently diminish the value of achievement itself. As trophies lined the shelves of children across the nation, the line between success and effort blurred. Children began to expect praise, not for excelling, but for simply existing.

For many in Generation X and Xenials, their upbringing had been defined by independence. They were often referred to as "latchkey kids," coming home from school to empty houses while their parents worked long hours. Left to their own devices, they learned to navigate life without constant adult supervision. On one hand, this instilled a sense of self-reliance. On the other, it left many feeling abandoned or neglected, forced to confront the world without guidance or support.

When they became parents, these generations swung the pendulum in the opposite direction. They vowed that their children would never feel the loneliness they had known. Enter the "helicopter parent," a term coined to describe the obsessive involvement of parents in every aspect of their children's lives. Instead of standing back and letting their kids figure things out on their own, these parents hovered, swooping in at the first sign of difficulty or conflict.

They handled everything from scheduling playdates and organizing school projects to mediating fights with friends. No challenge was too small for their intervention. If their child struggled in school, the parents would meet with the teachers to ensure that special accommodations were made. If their child was unhappy with a sports coach, they would demand changes. In their attempt to shield their kids from hardship, they effectively prevented them from learning how to solve problems independently.

This constant involvement in their children's lives left a generation of kids who were not only unaccustomed to solving their own problems but also deeply reliant on external validation. They grew up with the belief that the world should bend to their needs, just as their parents had done.

Alongside participation trophies and helicopter parenting, another subtle shift occurred: the culture of inclusivity at childhood events. Gone were the days when only the birthday child received presents. Now, every child at a birthday party walked away with a gift bag, no matter who's celebration it was. For Generation X and Xenial parents, this practice was seen as a way to ensure that no child ever felt left out or unimportant. Every child, they believed, deserved to feel special.

This mindset extended beyond birthday parties. Schools and community organizations began implementing policies where no child was excluded from activities or singled out for underperforming. Group rewards replaced individual ones, and the line between winners and losers was further erased.

To the parents of Generation Jones, X, and the Xenials, these changes seemed harmless, even kind. They wanted their children to grow up with higher self-esteem and a greater sense of belonging than they had known. However, what they didn't foresee was that these practices would lead to a generation that struggled to cope with the inevitable disappointments and inequities of adult life.

When Millennials and later generations, raised in this carefully curated environment, stepped into adulthood, the reality hit hard. Life wasn't handing out participation trophies. Relationships weren't as easy as receiving a gift bag for showing up, and the workplace was far less forgiving than the helicopter parents who had always intervened on their behalf.

Many young adults, unaccustomed to failure or rejection, found themselves unable to cope with the hardships of real life. They expected the world to cater to their needs, just as their parents had done, but quickly realized that the world didn't operate that way. Disillusionment set in. As jobs were lost, relationships fell apart, and student loans piled up, they struggled to understand why their lives weren't following the trajectory they had been promised.

And in that struggle, many turned their gaze backward, placing the blame on the very generations that had tried so hard to protect them. To them, it seemed as though Generation Jones, X, and the Xenials had created a world that shielded them from failure but left them unprepared for success. The participation trophies, the helicopter parenting, and the gift-giving culture had seemed like acts of love and care. But in the end, they had only delayed the inevitable lesson: life is hard, failure is real, and success must be earned.

What began as an effort to provide children with a better upbringing than their parents had experienced resulted in a generation ill-equipped for the real world. As the children of these generations confronted the difficulties of adulthood, the consequences of those well-meaning but misguided parenting choices became all too clear. The following story illustrates this reality.

When Emma turned eight, her birthday party was a celebration to behold. Balloons floated in the air, cake was piled high with frosting, and every child who attended left with a neatly wrapped gift, regardless of who the party was for. Emma didn't think twice about it. This was just how things were done. Everyone deserved to feel special, whether it was their day or not. And when the games ended, and the gifts and goodie bags were handed out, every kid got one, whether they had won or barely participated.

This was the world Emma and her friends were raised in. A world where effort was rewarded, regardless of the outcome. It wasn't just birthday parties. At school, sports, or dance recitals, there were no losers. Trophies lined shelves across her house, each one signifying not a victory, but the mere act of showing up. It felt good in the moment, safe, affirming, as though every step was a step in the right direction, whether it was earned or not.

As Emma grew older, the same message followed her: she was special, unique, and worthy of recognition simply for being herself. Her parents, ever vigilant, hovered closely, ready to swoop in at the first sign of trouble. Homework too hard? They'd have a word with the teacher. Disagreements with friends? They'd step in to mediate. Life, for Emma, was carefully padded, every challenge cushioned to minimize discomfort. Helicopter parenting, they called it. But Emma just called it normal.

She wasn't alone. An entire generation grew up this way, shielded from failure, disappointment, or the harsh edges of life. Emma's peers had similar experiences, where their every milestone was celebrated, and struggles were softened. But what Emma didn't realize was that this bubble of protection couldn't last forever.

The transition into adulthood was jarring. Emma graduated from college and entered a job market that wasn't interested in participation trophies. Her first performance review didn't end with a pat on the back just for trying. Instead, she was met with criticism, real, pointed feedback that rattled her confidence. She wasn't used to this. In her mind, effort alone should have been enough. But her employer wasn't impressed by how hard she tried. They wanted results.

Emma found that relationships, too, weren't as easy as they had once seemed. Friends, colleagues, and partners had expectations, and conflicts didn't come with a parental mediator to smooth things over. Disagreements weren't met with instant validation but often with indifference or challenge.

For the first time, Emma faced the uncomfortable truth that the world wasn't going to bend to her feelings. It didn't care if she felt special. Life had winners and losers, and the stakes were higher than any childhood game.

Her story mirrored that of many of her peers. Raised in a cocoon of constant affirmation and shielded from discomfort, Millennials and later generations found themselves unprepared for the realities of adulthood. Life wasn't handing out trophies anymore. Bills piled up, job markets were competitive, and the economy was far less forgiving than the classrooms and sports fields of their youth. Relationships were messy, and sometimes, no matter how hard you worked or how much you cared, things fell apart.

Emma began to feel a gnawing frustration. Why hadn't anyone told her it would be this hard? Why hadn't her parents, teachers, or society prepared her for a world where effort didn't always translate into success? The more she thought about it, the more she found herself blaming those who had come before her, the Baby Boomers, her parents, the very generation that had built the soft walls around her world.

Emma wasn't alone in her disillusionment. Across social media, in coffee shops, and in countless conversations with friends, a common refrain emerged: it wasn't supposed to be this way. How could previous generations have been so blind? How could they leave them to deal with crumbling economies, political divisions, and the sheer weight of adult responsibilities they hadn't been prepared for? It felt unfair, as though they had been handed a broken system and told to make the best of it.

Many felt that the Baby Boomers had it easy, stable jobs, affordable homes, and clear paths to success. But now, Millennials were saddled with student debt, skyrocketing rent prices, and jobs that no longer guaranteed security or upward mobility. To Emma and her peers, it seemed like the older generations had enjoyed the fruits of their labor but had left nothing behind for those who followed. It was easier to place the blame on them than to confront the uncomfortable reality that no amount of participation trophies or parental intervention could have shielded them from life's inevitable challenges.

As the frustrations of adulthood deepened, so did the generational divide. Baby Boomers, who had grown up with a different set of values, couldn't understand the complaints of the younger generations. To them, hardship and sacrifice were a normal part of life, even expected. Many had started working as teenagers, faced tough economic times, and built their futures from the ground up. They didn't see their own upbringing as cushioned or unfair; they saw it as a necessity. They had adapted and thrived, and they expected their children to do the same.

But for Millennials, like Emma, it felt different. They had been promised a world of endless opportunity, where hard work would guarantee success, just as it had for their parents. Yet, when they entered adulthood, they found the landscape had shifted beneath their feet. The participation trophies they had been given in childhood seemed like hollow tokens now, symbols of a world that had been more interested in protecting their feelings than preparing them for reality.

As Emma sat with her friends one evening, lamenting the state of their lives, one of them finally said what no one had wanted to admit. "Maybe we've been looking at this all wrong. Maybe... it was never supposed to be easy."

The room fell silent. They all knew, deep down, that the world wasn't going to change just because they wanted it to. Life wasn't going to hand out trophies for participation anymore. The harsh realities of adulthood weren't going to soften. If anything, the world was harder now than it had been for their parents. But blaming others wasn't going to fix that.

Emma realized that, just as her parents had to forge their path, she would have to forge hers. The participation trophies were long gone, and the safety net of her childhood had been pulled away. The world wasn't going to coddle her, but it had never been meant to.

The reckoning came slowly, but it came. Emma and her peers, raised on the belief that they were special just for showing up, began to understand that the only real way forward was to stop waiting for someone to make life easier and to start facing its challenges head-on. There would be no more trophies just for trying. But there might be real success for those willing to embrace the struggle.

CHAPTER FOUR
The Entitled Generations

As the new millennium dawned, the professional world began to change. Generation X, known for their independence and resilience, and Millennials, raised on the promise of endless opportunity, began to step into leadership roles across corporate, community, and government sectors.

For decades, the Baby Boomers and Gen Jones had held these positions, shaping institutions through values like hard work, competition, and personal responsibility. But now, as the Boomers started to retire, the mantle of leadership passed to a different set of hands—those of Gen X and Millennials, each with their own unique approach.

The Gen X Leaders, born between 1965 and 1980, had always been defined by their self-sufficiency. They were the "latchkey kids," raised in an era where both parents worked, or single-parent households were becoming more common. As a result, they grew up with a strong sense of independence and learned early how to navigate life's challenges with little help from authority figures. They embraced pragmatism over idealism and tended to shy away from the spotlight, preferring to let their results speak for themselves.

As Gen Xers began stepping into leadership roles, their approach was cautious but effective. Take Linda, for example. She grew up in the 1970s, spending many afternoons alone after school, making her own decisions from a young age. When she became the CEO of a mid-sized tech company, her leadership style reflected her upbringing. She fostered a culture of autonomy, encouraging employees to solve problems on their own, just as she had done growing up. Meetings were concise, with a focus on practical outcomes rather than lofty visions. Employees knew Linda would support them, but she wouldn't hold their hands. If they failed, they'd learn from it. This created a sense of accountability and trust within the company, traits that mirrored her generation's values.

Gen Xers like Linda led with a "get it done" attitude. In government, they were less concerned with grandstanding and more focused on pragmatic policy changes. They often steered clear of the idealistic rhetoric of Boomers and Millennials, focusing instead on practical solutions. John, a Gen X mayor in a growing city, exemplified this when he pushed through infrastructure updates that had been delayed for years. Rather than launching a grand, flashy initiative, he methodically worked behind the scenes, cutting red tape and ensuring that projects were completed on time and within budget. It wasn't glamorous, but it was effective.

While Gen X approached leadership with pragmatism, Millennials, born between 1981 and 1996, brought a different flavor. Raised on the idea that they were destined to change the world, Millennials entered leadership roles with a sense of purpose and little regard for history. They emphasized collaboration, transparency, and social responsibility, values that had been drilled into them from a young age.

Alex, a Millennial entrepreneur, built his entire company around the idea of doing well by doing good. His marketing agency, which catered to eco-conscious businesses, made social responsibility its core value. Employees were encouraged to collaborate, with open-office layouts and a flat organizational structure. There were no private offices. Alex believed in breaking down hierarchies to foster innovation. Decisions were made by committee, and the company's impact on the environment and community was as important as its profit margins. Under Alex's leadership, the company thrived, attracting like-minded talent and clients eager to align themselves with its values.

In government, Millennials brought similar ideals. Emily, a Millennial city councilwoman, pushed for more transparency in local government. She spearheaded initiatives that allowed citizens to have direct input into budgeting decisions and made sure meetings were live-streamed for public viewing. Her approach was less about traditional leadership and more about creating a sense of shared ownership between government and the community. While this openness usually slowed decision-making, it also increased civic engagement, especially among younger voters who had previously felt disconnected from the process.

But as Gen X and Millennials stepped into leadership roles, the generational tensions didn't fade. For many Gen Yers, also known as Zoomers, like Pop's grandson Eric, a young man struggling to find his way, the disillusionment with the world around them remained palpable. Born between the late 1990s and early 2010s, Gen Y came of age in a world shaped by economic instability, climate concerns, and political division. Unlike their predecessors, who had found ways to adapt, Gen Y often felt like the rug had been pulled out from under them.

Eric had graduated from college in 2020, right into the chaos of a global pandemic. Jobs were scarce, and the economy was unpredictable. He watched as older generations—the Boomers, Gen Xers, and even Millennials—seemed to hold the reins of power, and yet, in his mind, they had left behind a broken world. Housing prices were skyrocketing, student loan debt was crushing, and climate change loomed like a ticking time bomb. To Eric, it seemed like every problem his generation faced could be traced back to the decisions of those who came before him.

As he sat in his small apartment, scrolling through social media, Eric saw countless posts from his peers echoing his frustrations. Many blamed Baby Boomers specifically, citing their decades of control in business and government. It wasn't just about the economy; it was about the entire system. Boomers had grown up in a world where hard work led to home ownership, a stable career, and upward mobility. But Eric's reality was different. Despite his degree, he was stuck in a cycle of temporary jobs, unable to get a foothold in the professional world because employers would not conform to his expectations and regard him as an equal. He felt abandoned, left to deal with the consequences of previous generations' choices.

His discontent didn't end with the Boomers. Even as Gen Xers and Millennials rose into leadership positions, Eric and many of his peers felt they were still dealing with the fallout. Eric would often lament, "They're all part of the same system." He couldn't understand why Gen X leaders, who had grown up with struggles of their own, seemed to perpetuate a corporate culture that demanded results without fully acknowledging the obstacles Gen Y faced. Even the Millennials, with their collaborative and socially conscious approaches, seemed to have forgotten what it was like to be on the bottom rung of the ladder, trying to climb up in a world that felt rigged.

As Gen X and Millennials solidified their roles as the new leaders of industries and communities, the disconnection between generations deepened. Gen X leaders, with their "figure it out" mentality, couldn't fully understand why Gen Yers like Eric struggled to cope with challenges. To previous generations, failure was a natural part of life, a lesson they had learned early on. They didn't see the need to coddle the younger generation.

Millennials, for all their emphasis on collaboration and transparency, found it difficult to bridge the gap between their own optimism and the disillusionment felt by Gen Y. Many Millennials had entered the workforce during the 2008 financial crisis, but they had adapted. Now, they were in leadership roles, implementing policies that they believed would change the world. But to Eric, it all felt distant. He wanted tangible solutions to the problems he faced right now—student debt forgiveness, affordable housing, and stable job markets.

The irony was that as Eric and his peers blamed the generations before them, they were often unaware of the complexities that Boomers, Gen X and Millennials faced as leaders. While Gen Y searched for someone to blame, those in power were trying, in their own ways, to navigate an increasingly complex world—one filled with economic challenges, climate threats, and the weight of expectations from all sides.

The leadership of Gen X and Millennials, for all its purported progress, still hadn't found a way to fully reconcile the frustrations of Gen Y. The disconnect between these generations reflected a deeper societal issue of the struggle to balance the legacies of the past with the demands of the present, all while preparing for an uncertain future.

CHAPTER FIVE
Blaming the Builders

As Generation X, Millennials, Gen Y, and even Gen Z began to assume leadership roles across corporate, community, and government sectors, a noticeable trend emerged, one that was defined by a paradoxical disconnect.

These generations, equipped with modern ideals of inclusivity, collaboration, and innovation, were quick to dismiss the lessons of history, particularly those shaped by the Baby Boomers and earlier generations. For many, the world they had inherited seemed flawed, outdated, and in desperate need of change. Yet, in their eagerness to critique the past, they often failed to recognize that the very systems they thrived in were built by those same generations they now blamed for their struggles.

Generation X, born between 1965 and 1980, had long been described as pragmatic, independent, and skeptical of authority. When they began entering leadership positions, they brought with them an approach that valued results over process. But in their quest to modernize systems and streamline operations, many Gen Xers overlooked the foundation laid by previous generations. For them, the past was something to be overcome, not something to build upon.

Take Mike, a mid-level manager at a Fortune 500 company. Growing up in the 1980s, Mike had seen firsthand the rise of technology, globalization, and corporate restructuring. When he became a leader in his company, he quickly implemented new, tech-driven processes that drastically increased efficiency. However, Mike had little appreciation for the slow, steady groundwork laid by Boomers who had built the company from the ground up, brick by brick. He saw their methods as outdated, ignoring the fact that it was those methods that had sustained the company through economic recessions, oil crises, and shifts in global markets. In his eyes, the company's longevity wasn't thanks to their foresight, but rather by luck, despite their old-fashioned ways.

When Mike pushed for aggressive expansion into international markets without considering the company's historical caution, the plan backfired. A few key mistakes, overreliance on new technology, neglecting cultural nuances, cost the company millions. In the aftermath, Mike and his peers blamed "old-school thinking" for not adapting faster. Yet they missed the reality that the company's very existence was due to the conservative, risk-averse strategies of the Boomers who had weathered far worse storms.

Millennials, born between 1981 and 1996, often saw themselves as change-makers, destined to fix the flaws they believed older generations had created. Armed with ideals of collaboration, social justice, and rapid innovation, they entered leadership roles with a sense of urgency. However, their impatience often led them to overlook the complexity of the same world they were trying to reform.

Take Jessica, a Millennial city councilwoman who rose to prominence during her town's push for renewable energy. Passionate about combating climate change, Jessica led an ambitious initiative to transition her city's energy grid to solar and wind power within five years. On paper, the plan was revolutionary, but in practice, it lacked the infrastructure support and financial sustainability that previous generations had carefully balanced over decades.

In her pursuit of rapid change, Jessica dismissed the wisdom of older engineers and city planners who warned that the existing grid wasn't equipped for such a swift overhaul. They had been through energy crises in the past and knew the risks of moving too quickly without sufficient backup systems. But to Jessica, these concerns were just more examples of outdated thinking. "They don't understand the urgency," she would say.

When the city experienced frequent blackouts during the winter due to the unreliable transition, Jessica and her colleagues were left scrambling for solutions. The blame, however, wasn't placed on their rushed plan, it was placed on the infrastructure "inherited" from the Boomers, infrastructure they saw as obsolete. What they didn't grasp or appreciate was that this same infrastructure had provided steady, reliable energy for decades, despite its limitations.

Gen Y, or Zoomers, born between the late 1990s and early 2010s, were the most vocal in their frustration with the world they had inherited. Coming of age in the shadow of financial crises, political polarization, and a global pandemic, many felt they had been handed a broken system. Unlike Gen X or Millennials, who had seen the world shift before their eyes, Gen Y was born into uncertainty, and their disillusionment was palpable.

Quintrell, a protégé of Barak Obama, and a young community organizer, embodied this sentiment. Frustrated by rising inequality and stagnant wages, he organized protests and campaigns aimed at addressing what he believed were systemic failures created by Baby Boomers and perpetuated by Gen X and Millennials. "They've left us nothing," he often told his peers. "The world is falling apart because they refused to fix it."

But Quintrell and his peers failed to see the strides previous generations had made to build a world where such activism could even exist. The very freedoms and platforms they used to voice their dissent were products of decades of struggle for civil rights, workers' protections, and economic reforms.

Boomers had fought for voting rights, for environmental regulations, for opportunities that previous generations never had. Yet, to Quintrell, these accomplishments were invisible, overshadowed by what he saw as failures. He didn't see that the world he wanted to change had been built, brick by brick, by people who had faced even greater challenges.

When Quintrell's community movement faltered due to logistical and funding problems, he blamed the "outdated" systems in place. What he couldn't grasp was that those very systems, while imperfect, had been meticulously designed by earlier generations to balance ambition with practicality, change with stability.

Generation Z, born after 2012, brought an entirely new dynamic to leadership. Raised with the internet and social media as a constant presence, Gen Z had access to more information than any generation before them. Yet, in many ways, this access came at the expense of understanding history. Gen Z leaders were quick to embrace digital solutions, often assuming that newer was always better. But without a foundational grasp of the lessons from the past, their innovations sometimes lacked the depth of understanding necessary for long-term success.

Taylor, a Gen Z entrepreneur, built a highly successful startup focused on decentralized finance (DeFi). He and his team prided themselves on being disruptors, eager to bypass traditional banking systems, which they viewed as relics of an outdated world. "Banks are slow, inefficient, and stuck in the past," Taylor often said. To him, the boomers who had built the banking system didn't understand the digital age and had failed to adapt.

But when a sudden market downturn occurred, Taylor's company, which had scaled rapidly without sufficient safeguards, collapsed. As investors pulled out and regulations tightened, Taylor blamed the "legacy" banking system for his company's failure, accusing it of being out of touch with the modern financial landscape. Yet, Taylor didn't acknowledge that it was the very regulations and safeguards put in place by previous generations—following their own financial disasters—that had sustained the global economy for so long.

Additionally, Taylor's reliance on digital and cloud-based operations, like that of many Gen Z entrepreneurs, reflects a broader generational trend of embracing new technologies without fully understanding their vulnerabilities.

Gen Z, having grown up in an era dominated by the internet, social media, and mobile apps, views the digital landscape as not just convenient, but essential. For many, it's an integral part of their professional and personal lives, offering seemingly limitless possibilities for growth and innovation. However, this reliance on cloud-based systems and digital infrastructure has unwittingly created a buffet for identity thieves and cybercriminals.

In Taylor's case, his DeFi (decentralized finance) company operated almost entirely in the digital sphere. Like many other Gen Z leaders, Taylor saw cloud-based operations as the future of business: fast, flexible, and globally accessible. He trusted the technology to handle financial transactions, store sensitive customer data, and manage day-to-day operations.

The allure of scalability, the ease of use, and the cost savings over traditional banking and data storage systems made cloud technology irresistible. Unfortunately, it also came with significant risks that Taylor, like many others without a concept of history, failed to fully appreciate.

While cloud-based systems offer numerous advantages, they are also vulnerable to hacking, data breaches, and cyberattacks. Cybercriminals, especially identity thieves, are well aware of this. The more digital platforms like Taylor's rely on the cloud for storing customer data, financial records, and personal information, the more attractive they become to hackers.

The very accessibility and convenience that make the cloud appealing to companies also make it a prime target. For example, Taylor's company handled financial transactions using blockchain technology and stored customer information in the cloud.

However, as a Gen Z entrepreneur focused on growth and innovation, he did not invest heavily in cybersecurity measures. Many startups and digital-native companies, eager to scale quickly, prioritize user experience and rapid expansion over security infrastructure. Taylor's assumption that newer technology was inherently more secure than legacy systems turned out to be a dangerous miscalculation.

One of the key issues with the digital-first mindset embraced by Gen Z is the failure to learn from previous generations' focus on safeguarding assets. Older generations, especially the Boomers, had to grapple with traditional security concerns like physical theft, fraud, and paper-based vulnerabilities. But they also built systems of checks and balances, including extensive regulatory frameworks, to minimize these risks.

Gen Z, however, often views these systems as outdated, failing to see the necessity of translating those safeguards into the digital realm. Taylor, for instance, may have viewed traditional financial institutions as slow and inefficient, but those institutions have spent decades developing robust cybersecurity protocols to protect customers' identities and data. In their eagerness to disrupt the status quo, Gen Z leaders sometimes overlook the vital importance of strong security measures in favor of speed and accessibility.

Without sufficient encryption protocols, multi-factor authentication, or routine security audits, Taylor's business was vulnerable. A hacker easily exploited a weak link in his company's cloud storage system, gaining access to thousands of users' personal data—names, social security numbers, financial information—all of which could be sold on the dark web or used for identity theft. This creates a snowball effect, as once sensitive information is exposed, it can be exploited multiple times, leaving victims dealing with the fallout for years.

For businesses like Taylor's, the fallout is equally severe. Beyond the immediate financial loss from a data breach, the long-term damage to reputation can be fatal. Customers lose trust in companies that fail to protect their personal information, leading to a loss of clients, a drop in revenue, and potential legal consequences. Across corporate, community, and government leadership roles, these generational shift revealed a common thread—a lack of historical perspective.

Gen Xers, Millennials, Gen Y, and Gen Z all shared a tendency to critique the systems they had inherited without fully understanding the complexities behind them. They viewed the world as something to be fixed, failing to recognize that it had been built by the very generations they blamed for their own struggles.

The truth was, the Baby Boomers and earlier generations had built a world out of necessity, often out of survival. They had faced wars, recessions, political upheavals, and social revolutions. Each challenge had shaped the systems, institutions, and industries that now sustained modern life.

While those systems were not perfect, they had been created by people who had lived through far more turmoil than many younger generations could imagine. The irony is that the very stability that allows Gen X, Millennials, Gen Y, and Gen Z to critique, innovate, and lead is the product of the hard-won lessons of history.

In the end, the failure to appreciate the past left these generations repeating mistakes their predecessors had already encountered. The dismissal of history, coupled with the belief that everything old was obsolete, led to a cycle of disillusionment, where each new generation blamed the one before for their struggles. And in that blame, they overlooked a fundamental truth: the world they lived in had been built by the very people they now dismissed.

CHAPTER SIX
The Mischaracterization of Boomers, Gen Jones, and Early Gen Xers as the Enemy

In the past decade, a growing cultural divide has emerged between older generations, particularly Baby Boomers, Generation Jones (those born between Boomers and Gen X), and early Gen Xers, and younger generations, including Millennials, Gen Y, and Gen Z. Many younger people often see their elders as obstacles to progress, outdated relics of a society they feel is ill-equipped to meet the challenges of the modern world.

Yet, in their eagerness to push for rapid change, these younger generations often lack an understanding and appreciation of the historical context that shaped the values and systems they are so quick to critique. This gap in understanding has created a distorted narrative where older generations are framed as the enemies of progress, a perception driven more by frustration than historical insight.

The Baby Boomer generation, born between 1946 and 1964, is frequently cast as the chief antagonist in this generational conflict. Many Millennials, Gen Y, and Gen Zers see Boomers as the generation that "had it all"—affordable education, job security, and a stable housing market—yet squandered these advantages and left behind a planet struggling with climate change, political instability, and economic inequality. The now-common phrase "OK Boomer," used by younger generations to dismiss what they view as outdated opinions, encapsulates the frustration many feel toward this older generation.

An example of this generational conflict occurred in 2019, when Greta Thunberg, the young Swedish climate activist, gave her famous speech at the United Nations, accusing older generations of stealing her future by failing to act on climate change. While her message was powerful and undeniably urgent, the blame was squarely placed on Boomers for their supposed inaction. Yet, this narrative overlooks the fact that many of the environmental protections in place today—such as the Clean Air Act and the Environmental Protection Agency in the United States—were spearheaded by Boomers who fought for change during the 1960s and 1970s.

This mischaracterization of Boomers as enemies of progress is not entirely new. What has changed, however, is the intensity of the blame being placed on them for systemic issues that have roots in global economic and political systems beyond the control of any single generation. Younger people frustrated with perceived climate inaction, unaffordable housing, and student debt tend to view Boomers as selfish and out of touch, when in reality, many Boomers fought against these very problems, albeit in a different historical context.

Generation Jones, born between 1955 and 1965, often goes unnoticed in the broader generational conversation, overshadowed by both Boomers and Gen Xers has become another scapegoat and are frequently caught in the crossfire of criticism from younger generations. In recent years, Gen Jones has found themselves lumped in with Boomers and accused of contributing to the very problems that Millennials, Gen Y, and Gen Z feel they are now burdened with.

For example, in debates about student loan debt and the housing crisis, it is common for younger generations to argue that previous generations had it easier, citing lower tuition costs and affordable housing prices. Yet, many Gen Jonesers experienced the beginning of the economic shifts that led to today's crises. They lived through the 1980s when wages began to stagnate and wealth inequality grew. Many struggled with economic uncertainty and rising costs, but this historical context is often overlooked by younger critics who paint them with the same broad brush as Boomers.

In the tech industry, for instance, many influential Gen Jonesers helped lay the foundation for the digital world that Millennials and Gen Z now take for granted. Steve Jobs and Bill Gates, both part of Generation Jones, revolutionized technology and computing, yet their contributions are often disregarded in favor of critiquing the industries that younger generations believe have not done enough to address social and environmental issues.

While Gen Jonesers played a key role in creating the modern technological landscape, their efforts are often overshadowed by criticisms of the corporate structures that later arose around those innovations.

Early Gen Xers, born between 1965 and 1975, are also frequently characterized as resistant to change by younger generations. Initially dubbed the "slacker generation" for their perceived apathy during the 1980s and 1990s, Gen Xers are now viewed by many Millennials and Gen Zers as part of the establishment they feel is holding back progress.

One stark example of this occurred during the height of the Black Lives Matter protests in 2020. Many younger activists expressed frustration with Gen X leaders in corporate and government positions, accusing them of not being radical enough in their approach to issues like racial justice and police reform.

Early Gen Xers, who had been shaped by the cynicism of the post-Vietnam and Watergate era, were more likely to seek incremental change and compromise. To younger activists, this approach seemed passive and outdated, leading to generational clashes in how to best address perceived systemic racism.

This lack of appreciation for the historical context in which Gen Xers grew up is apparent in the workplace as well. As many Gen Xers moved into management roles, they found themselves at odds with Millennials and Gen Zers who demanded more flexible work arrangements, rapid career advancement regardless of talent or skill, and a greater emphasis on work-life balance.

What younger generations often fail to recognize is that Gen Xers were the first to experience the shift toward a more precarious, less secure job market. Many worked through economic recessions and layoffs in the 1990s and early 2000s, leaving them more cautious about radical workplace reforms.

The generational friction that characterizes today's cultural and political discourse is, in part, a result of a lack of historical perspective among younger generations. Millennials, Gen Y, and Gen Z often view older generations as relics of a bygone era, disconnected from the realities of modern life. Yet, these younger generations frequently misunderstand and fail to appreciate the challenges their elders faced and the progress they made within the constraints of their own time.

For instance, younger generations may criticize Boomers and early Gen Xers for their perceived resistance to progressive social policies, without acknowledging the strides those generations made in advancing civil rights, women's rights, and LGBTQ+ rights. The passage of the Civil Rights Act, Roe v. Wade, and the establishment of Title IX were all battles fought by these older generations. While Millennials, Gen Y, and Gen Z continue to push for further progress, they sometimes fail to appreciate the foundation of change that was laid by those before them.

The tension between younger and older generations often stems from a false dichotomy that pits progress against preservation. Younger generations are understandably eager to push for rapid change in areas such as climate policy, social justice, and economic reform, but they often do so with a mindset that sees older generations as enemies of progress.

In reality, Boomers, Gen Jones, and early Gen Xers are not universally opposed to change. They simply have a different understanding of how change happens, informed by the historical challenges they faced.

In the rush to critique the past, younger generations risk overlooking the wisdom and hard-won experience that older generations possess. Dismissing Boomers, Gen Jonesers, and early Gen Xers as "enemies of progress" not only creates unnecessary division, but it also prevents a deeper understanding of how the past informs the present. The very systems and freedoms that Millennials, Gen Y, and Gen Z now enjoy—whether it's the technological infrastructure, environmental protections, or social movements, were often built by the generations they now criticize.

CHAPTER SEVEN
Defending Their Legacy

As the cultural and generational divide deepens, Baby Boomers, Generation Jones, and early Gen Xers increasingly find themselves under fire from younger generations. The younger cohorts often mischaracterize their elders as the primary obstacles to progress and personal success, blaming them for economic hardships, environmental crises, and perceived social injustices.

This widespread misperception, however, is not simply a product of generational differences but a consequence of how younger generations were raised, conditioned to deflect responsibility for their own circumstances. This narrative of blame has placed older generations on the defensive, compelling them to protect what they've spent their lives building from being unfairly dismantled.

Millennials and younger generations have come of age in a cultural environment marked by a shift in parenting and educational philosophies. Participation trophies, helicopter parenting, and an increasing emphasis on shielding children from failure have contributed to a mentality that often absolves younger people from personal accountability.

Instead of being taught that life's setbacks are natural challenges to overcome, many were conditioned to view failure as something unfairly imposed by external forces. This upbringing, while often well-meaning, created a generation that expects success to be handed to them and tends to place blame on others when life doesn't go as planned.

For example, in the context of the job market, Millennials and Gen Zers frequently argue that older generations created a broken system, leading to high levels of student debt, stagnant wages, and unaffordable housing. While these are real issues, the narrative often ignores the fact that Boomers, Gen Jonesers, and early Gen Xers also faced economic challenges unique to their time.

They dealt with inflation, recessions, and corporate downsizing, yet managed to build careers and homes through hard work and adaptability. However, this history is largely forgotten or dismissed by younger generations, who were raised with the idea that systemic obstacles are the primary reason for their struggles, rather than individual choices and resilience.

This conditioning against personal accountability manifests in how younger generations interpret their life circumstances. Instead of viewing challenges as part of the human experience, they often see them as failures of the older generations to provide a better world. As a result, Boomers, Gen Jones, and early Gen Xers are seen not as builders or contributors to progress, but as impediments to the success of the younger generations.

This ongoing narrative of blame has naturally put the older generations in a defensive posture. After spending their lives building the very systems that allow younger people to thrive, whether in technology, civil rights, or environmental protections, Boomers, Gen Jonesers, and early Gen Xers feel unfairly attacked. For many, it's not just a matter of being criticized for societal shortcomings; it's a feeling that everything they worked for is being discounted or, worse, threatened with destruction.

Consider the advances in technology that shape the world today. Many Boomers and early Gen Xers pioneered the tech revolution, laying the foundation for the digital age. Yet, younger generations often focus on how large tech companies exacerbate inequality or invade privacy, without recognizing the monumental contributions their predecessors made to connect the world and expand access to information. To these older generations, the hostility toward what they helped create feels not only ungrateful but as if their legacy is being unfairly tarnished.

Moreover, on issues like climate change and social justice, Boomers and Gen Jonesers often find themselves caricatured as indifferent or resistant to progress. Younger generations see them as having ignored the warning signs of environmental collapse or clinging to outdated social norms.

However, older generations were the ones who initiated the first waves of environmental legislation, civil rights movements, and feminist advances that opened the door for the further progress that Millennials and Gen Z continue to push for today.

When Boomers, Gen Jones, and early Gen Xers defend their choices and legacy, it's not out of an unwillingness to acknowledge current problems; rather, they fear seeing their life's work dismissed, eroded, or undone by younger people who lack a broader understanding of the challenges they faced and the progress they made.

The root of this defensive posture lies in a fundamental disconnect between generations. Younger people, conditioned to see life's hardships as the result of someone else's actions, whether systemic, political, or generational, often lack an appreciation for the incremental progress made over time. Older generations, by contrast, were taught that success and failure are deeply personal experiences. They saw themselves as agents of their own futures, even when faced with systemic obstacles like economic downturns, wars, or social upheavals.

For Boomers, Gen Jonesers, and early Gen Xers, the idea that they are being blamed for problems like student debt, climate change, or political instability can be deeply frustrating. These generations grew up in a world where personal responsibility was a cornerstone of adulthood, and they were taught to confront life's challenges head-on.

They made sacrifices, adapted to difficult circumstances, and often worked long hours in jobs that offered less flexibility or security than today's workforce demands. From their perspective, the younger generations' tendency to assign blame to their elders reflects a lack of resilience and a failure to acknowledge that progress takes time, effort, and personal accountability.

For instance, when younger generations blame Boomers for the student debt crisis, they often overlook the fact that higher education was more affordable in the past because government funding and policies, crafted by Boomers themselves, made it so. However, as state and federal funding for higher education decreased over time, tuition costs skyrocketed. Instead of recognizing the complexity of this issue, younger people frequently view it as a simple failure of older generations to "fix" the system for them, rather than as a consequence of broader economic and political forces.

This growing generational rift has led many Boomers, Gen Jonesers, and early Gen Xers to push back against the idea that they are enemies of progress. They see themselves as having fought for change, often in the face of greater adversity than younger generations realize. From civil rights marches to the environmental movement to the fight for LGBTQ+ equality, these generations were not idle bystanders in history—they were active participants in shaping the world.

Now, as they see younger generations criticizing the systems they helped build, older generations are compelled to defend their legacy. They worry that the eagerness of Millennials, Gen Y, and Gen Z to tear down institutions they view as flawed will result in the loss of hard-won progress. For example, many Boomers and early Gen Xers see the push for rapid political and economic reform as shortsighted, fearing that sweeping changes without careful consideration could lead to instability as it historically has.

This concern is not about resistance to change but about preserving the core principles that have made society functional: hard work, personal responsibility, and the understanding that progress is often incremental, not instantaneous. To many older generations, the younger generations' demand for immediate solutions without an appreciation for the complexities involved is not just unrealistic. It's dangerous.

CHAPTER EIGHT
Generations of Complaint and Comfort

Generations Y and Z, born into a world of rapid technological progress, have become vocal critics of the current state of society, frequently expressing dissatisfaction with issues ranging from economic inequality to environmental degradation to social justice. Their concerns are, in many cases, valid, and their activism has brought necessary attention to important issues.

However, there is a striking paradox that emerges when observing their behavior: while Gen Y and Zers loudly decry the shortcomings of the world they've inherited, they seem unwilling to forgo the very comforts, technologies, and freedoms that were developed by the generations they blame.

One of the clearest examples of this paradox is the relationship Gen Y and Z have with technology. These generations have grown up in an era where the internet, smartphones, and instant access to information are seen as basic necessities, not luxuries. They use these tools to voice their concerns, often loudly and publicly, about the state of the world. Platforms like Twitter, TikTok, and Instagram have become central to their activism, with users spreading awareness about climate change, racial injustice, and economic inequality.

However, these same platforms, and the underlying technology that makes them possible, are products of the very capitalist systems that Millennials and later generations often criticize. Take, for example, Jeff Bezos and Amazon. Bezos is a frequent target of Gen Y and Z anger, viewed as the epitome of wealth inequality and corporate exploitation. Yet, Amazon's same-day delivery service, its vast online marketplace, and its ubiquitous cloud infrastructure are widely used by the same individuals who condemn Bezos' wealth. Let's take a closer look at this paradox.

While specific breakdowns of Amazon's customer demographics aren't always publicly available, studies and surveys provide estimates of the percentage of Amazon's customer base made up by Gen Y and Gen Z. Millennials (Gen Y) are a significant portion of Amazon's customer base. Estimates suggest that Millennials make up approximately 30-35% of Amazon's U.S. customer base. This makes sense, as Millennials are digital natives and frequently use e-commerce platforms for both convenience and price comparison.

Gen Z, typically defined as those born from 1997 to the early 2010s, is also an important and growing demographic for Amazon. Although their share is smaller compared to Millennials, as younger people are just entering the workforce, they are expected to represent about 10-15% of

Amazon's customers in the U.S. Gen Z tends to prefer online shopping and is particularly responsive to fast delivery and personalized shopping experiences.

Together, Millennials and Gen Z likely make up around 40-50% of Amazon's customer base, driven by their digital fluency and preference for online shopping.

During the height of the COVID-19 pandemic, when many were calling for a reevaluation of corporate power and the distribution of wealth, Millennials and Gen Zers also leaned heavily on Amazon to provide them with the products and services they needed while stuck at home. The outcry against Amazon's labor practices was loud, yet the convenience of quick deliveries and access to almost any product online ensured that few were willing to completely boycott the company.

Millennials and Gen Zers also rail against perceived environmental degradation, often accusing older generations of having failed to protect the planet. Movements like Fridays for Future, led by Gen Z activist Greta Thunberg, have pushed for dramatic changes in the way the world approaches energy consumption, fossil fuels, and industrial development. Yet, while Gen Y and Zers may participate in climate marches and post their concerns online, they are deeply embedded in, and completely reliant upon, the very infrastructure they condemn.

For example, Millennials and Gen Zers frequently call for an end to fossil fuels, but they are largely unwilling to make the lifestyle changes that would be required if society suddenly abandoned these energy sources. Most still drive gas-powered cars or rely on public transportation systems that run on oil, and few seem willing to give up the electricity that powers their homes, offices, and devices. Much of which still comes from coal, oil, or natural gas.

Young pro-climate activists in their twenties joyfully attend a climate rally, holding a signs that say "End Fossil Fuels Now," only to later hop into their gasoline powered cars for a road trip across the country to another protest. Similarly, college students might use their laptops, charged by energy derived from fossil fuels, to write papers decrying the lack of action on climate change. The reality is that the infrastructure supporting their everyday lives, highways, power grids, manufacturing, was built by the very systems they want to dismantle, yet they remain unwilling to give up the conveniences those systems provide.

Meet Jack, a 28-year-old Millennial frustrated with the state of the world. Every day, his social media feeds were flooded with stories about economic inequality, climate change, and political corruption. It felt like the world was falling apart, and Jack was convinced that it was the fault of the older generations. He often voiced his complaints to anyone who would listen.

"The Boomers and Gen Xers screwed us over," Jack would say. "They built this broken system, and now we're the ones stuck with the consequences." He was particularly fed up with the environmental damage caused by fossil fuels and the unchecked corporate greed of tech billionaires. He believed that if his generation had been in charge all along, things would be different. Life would be fairer, greener, and more sustainable.

One night, after another rant at a gathering of friends, one of them, tired of Jack's constant complaints, challenged him. "Okay, if you hate what the older generations have created so much, why don't you try living without any of it? No tech, no products, nothing that was created before the year 2000. And nothing built with fossil fuels."

Jack scoffed at the suggestion, but his pride got the better of him. "Fine," he said. "I'll do it. I'll show you that I don't need all this mess they created."

The next morning, Jack woke up and immediately realized how difficult this challenge would be. He couldn't check his phone. Smartphones were out of the question since they were created after 2000. He glanced over at his laptop but remembered that the internet, as he knew it, was a product of the late 1990s and beyond. He'd have to avoid that, too.

Without modern technology, Jack couldn't order food online or even use a microwave, since it wasn't clear how much of it relied on post-2000 technology or fossil fuel-powered supply chains. He had to walk to the local farmer's market, assuming they didn't use trucks powered by gasoline to deliver the goods. The walk itself was enlightening. His sneakers, made by one of the biggest global brands, were also likely created using synthetic materials derived from fossil fuels. He had to stop wearing them.

As the days passed, Jack's modern conveniences began to disappear. He couldn't use his car, as it ran on gasoline, a fossil fuel. He had to rely on a bicycle, but even that was questionable, as its parts were produced in factories that used fossil fuels. Eventually, he decided walking was safest, but it limited his ability to get around.

Cooking was another challenge. Most of his food was packaged and transported using modern technology and fossil-fuel-dependent systems. He resorted to eating what little he could find locally, mostly vegetables, grains, and the occasional egg from a nearby farm. Even then, he wasn't sure if the farm's machinery was fossil-fuel-free.

Without access to electricity generated by fossil fuels, Jack's evenings were spent in darkness or by candlelight. He had to give up his electric lights, his refrigerator, and his television. After a few days of living without these modern amenities, Jack began to feel isolated. He couldn't call or text friends, couldn't watch the latest shows, and couldn't even listen to music unless he found an old battery powered cassette player or record player.

By the end of the week, Jack was mentally and physically exhausted. His life, once filled with convenience and comfort, had become an endless string of small, tedious struggles. He hadn't realized how much his daily routine was shaped by the very things he had been complaining about, namely technology, fossil fuels, and the infrastructure built by previous generations.

Jack had learned the hard way that, while the world wasn't perfect, the technology, infrastructure, and systems built by previous generations provided an incredible amount of convenience and comfort. And while progress was necessary, tearing down what had been built without understanding its value wasn't the answer.

CHAPTER NINE
Economic Inequality

Another frequent target of Gen Y and Z frustration is economic inequality. Younger generations feel that the gap between the wealthy and the poor is growing wider, and that capitalism has created a system in which the ultra-wealthy benefit at the expense of the average person.

They point to billionaires like Elon Musk, Mark Zuckerberg, and Bill Gates as symbols of the problem. Social media feeds are filled with posts that decry the "billionaire class" and the vast accumulation of wealth among the elite. Yet, these same generations are ardent consumers of the products created by the companies these billionaires run. Apple, founded by Steve Jobs and Steve Wozniak and now led by Tim Cook, is one of the most successful tech companies in history. Millennials and Gen Zers eagerly purchase the latest iPhone models, despite the high price tags, because the sleek design, functionality, and status that come with owning Apple products are highly desirable.

Similarly, Tesla cars are a status symbol for environmentally conscious Millennials and Gen Zers, who often fail to acknowledge the irony of celebrating a product created by one of the very billionaires they criticize—Elon Musk. Tesla's electric cars are viewed as the future of green transportation, yet the company has faced accusations of poor labor practices, and Musk himself has been vilified for his wealth. Despite this, many in Gen Y and Z aspire to own a Tesla, seeing it as a badge of environmental responsibility.

The desire for the latest gadgets, clothing, and technology keeps younger generations deeply entangled in the capitalist structures they claim to oppose. While they may denounce the rise of fast fashion or the exploitation of workers in other countries, many Millennials and Gen Zers still buy affordable clothing from companies like Zara and H&M, justifying it as a necessity due to their limited budgets. This unwillingness to change their consumption habits undermines their calls for economic reform and highlights the deep contradictions in their beliefs and actions.

In addition to material comforts, Gen Y and Zers often take for granted the social freedoms they enjoy. They frequently protest for more expansive civil rights and social justice reforms, which are laudable causes, but they sometimes fail to appreciate the hard-fought battles that previous generations endured to secure the very rights they now take as a given.

For instance, Millennials and Gen Zers participate in online discussions and campaigns for equality, diversity, and inclusion. They advocate for the rights of marginalized groups, often pointing to the failures of previous generations to fully eradicate racism, sexism, and homophobia. Yet, they rarely acknowledge that the freedoms they now enjoy, freedom of speech, access to higher education, the right to protest, are the results of decades of activism and legislative victories secured by Baby Boomers and Gen Xers.

For example, the civil rights movement of the 1960s, led by figures like Martin Luther King Jr., resulted in landmark legislation that laid the groundwork for the social justice movements Millennials and Gen Zers now champion. Feminists of the 1970s fought for reproductive rights and workplace equality, while LGBTQ+ activists in the 1980s and 1990s pushed for marriage equality and legal protections.

These victories were not won overnight but required decades of perseverance, sacrifice, and struggle. However, younger generations often express frustration that progress isn't happening fast enough, without fully grasping the historical context that informs today's battles.

The paradox of Gen Y and Z is that, while they loudly decry the state of the world and criticize older generations for the problems they face, they are unwilling to give up the very comforts, technologies, and freedoms that were created by those same generations. They rally against capitalism while benefiting from its products, criticize the exploitation of workers while continuing to participate in consumer-driven economies, and demand social justice reforms without appreciating the progress made by previous generations.

Throughout history, each generation has tangibly contributed to the advancement of humanity, from groundbreaking inventions to life-saving medical developments. However, when comparing the achievements of pre-Millennial generations, such as the Silent Generation, Baby Boomers, and Generation X, with those of Millennials and Gen Z, a stark difference in the scale and nature of these contributions becomes evident.

While Millennials and Gen Z have harnessed technology in impressive ways, the foundation of modern society was largely built by the generations that preceded them. These earlier generations laid the groundwork for the digital age and the subsequent conveniences that later generations often take for granted.

The pre-Millennial generations were responsible for some of the most revolutionary advancements in history. The 20th century, dominated by the Silent Generation, Baby Boomers, and early Gen Xers, was a golden age of invention, driven by necessity, war, and the desire to solve humanity's most pressing challenges.

The Microchip (1959): Invented by Jack Kilby and Robert Noyce, the microchip became the foundation of modern electronics, from computers to smartphones. Without the microchip, there would be no internet, no personal computers, and no digital devices. The groundwork for everything from the PC revolution of the 1980s to the iPhone in 2007 was made possible by this one invention, a brainchild of Baby Boomers and Silent Generation scientists.

The Internet (1960s-1990s): The invention and development of the internet began in the 1960s, with ARPANET, funded by the U.S. Department of Defense. It was refined in the 1970s and 1980s by Baby Boomers and early Gen Xers. By the time the first website was launched in 1991, the groundwork for the World Wide Web had been firmly established by these pre-Millennial innovators.

Personal Computers (1970s-1980s): Pioneers like Steve Jobs, Steve Wozniak, and Bill Gates (all Boomers) transformed the bulky, inaccessible computers of the 1960s into the personal computers of the 1980s and 1990s. This innovation reshaped industries, workplaces, and homes, making computing power accessible to millions.

Space Exploration (1960s-1970s): The Apollo moon landing in 1969, a monumental achievement for humanity, was made possible by the ingenuity of pre-Millennial generations. Boomers and Silents led the way in space exploration, pushing the boundaries of science and technology. Today's space race, dominated by companies like SpaceX, led by Gen Xers like Elon Musk who wasn't born until 1971, is built upon the foundation laid by these early pioneers.

Vaccines (1950s-1980s): Pre-Millennial scientists developed some of the most important vaccines in history, eradicating diseases like smallpox and polio. Jonas Salk's polio vaccine (1955) and the later development of vaccines for measles, mumps, and rubella revolutionized public health. These breakthroughs saved millions of lives and laid the foundation for today's advancements in immunology.

Organ Transplants (1960s-1980s): The first successful organ transplant occurred in 1954, followed by the development of heart, liver, and kidney transplants in the 1960s and 1970s. Surgeons and researchers from pre-Millennial generations took medical science into uncharted territory, saving countless lives and pushing the boundaries of what was possible in the operating room.

MRI Machines (1977): The development of Magnetic Resonance Imaging (MRI) machines revolutionized diagnostic medicine. Gen X pioneers played a critical role in the commercialization of MRIs in the late 20th century, giving doctors an unprecedented view inside the human body.

These inventions were the result of visionaries who worked in an era of very limited computing power, minimal connectivity, and fewer resources. They were driven by the desire to solve large, systemic problems like wars, disease, and technological limitations. They fundamentally changed how we live, work, and interact with one another.

The sheer number of groundbreaking inventions by Millennials and Gen Z does not come close to the transformative technologies of previous generations. Later generations have simply reimagined the ways in which society interacts with technology. In many cases, they have simply built upon the foundation left by their predecessors.

Social Media (2000s): While the internet was created by Boomers and Gen Xers, Millennials and Gen Z transformed how the world uses it. While these platforms have reshaped how people connect and share information across the globe. They do not exist apart from the infrastructure built by the previous generations.

Similarly, the smartphone was built on pre-Millennial inventions like the microchip and mobile networks. Millennials and later generations simply popularized its use and drove its evolution from a novelty into a necessity.

Alternatively, CRISPR and Gene Editing (2010s): CRISPR technology, developed largely by Millennial and Gen Z scientists, has revolutionized genetics. This tool has allowed for precise gene editing that may eventually help cure genetic diseases, treat cancers, and according to GenZ ideology, potentially alter the future of human evolution. CRISPR is one of the most significant medical advancements in recent decades.

While earlier generations laid the groundwork for medical technology, Millennials and Gen Zers have accelerated the adoption of telemedicine. The COVID-19 pandemic saw a massive increase in remote healthcare services, powered by apps and online platforms. The widespread availability of health-monitoring apps and wearable technology like Fitbits and Apple Watches is also largely driven by younger generations.

Millennials and Gen Z have integrated AI into various sectors, including medicine. AI-driven diagnostic tools are enhancing the speed and accuracy of diagnoses, improving patient outcomes, and optimizing treatments. And as innovative as AI technology is, the hardware and infrastructure were invented and developed by previous generations.

CHAPTER TEN
Societal Advancement Takes Time, Sacrifice, and Accountability

John Harrison sat on the porch, his weathered hands resting on the arms of his rocking chair as he watched his grandson, Eric, pacing back and forth, frustration written all over his face. The sun was setting, casting a golden hue over the trees, but Eric was too preoccupied to notice.

"It's just… it feels like everything's falling apart," Eric said, finally stopping to face his grandfather. "The economy, the environment, politics, it's all a mess. And it's because of the decisions your generation made. You guys built this system, and now we're the ones who have to deal with it."

John didn't respond immediately. He took a deep breath, the cool evening air filling his lungs as he prepared himself to say what he'd been thinking for some time. Eric was a bright young man, full of passion and ideas, but he also carried a resentment John had noticed in many people of Eric's generation. It was a resentment born out of frustration, but it was directed at the wrong place.

You're right about one thing, Eric," John finally said, his voice calm but firm. "My generation, and the ones before mine, did build the world you live in. But what you don't see is that the world we built wasn't perfect, and it wasn't without challenges. But it was necessary for the progress we've made, and it gave your generation a platform to advance even further."

Eric's brow furrowed. "But look at where we are. The environment is in crisis, the economy is rigged against regular people, and the political system doesn't work. How is that progress?" John nodded. "I understand why you're upset. But before you write off everything that came before you, let me tell you a story."

John leaned forward in his chair, resting his elbows on his knees. "When I was your age, we didn't have the conveniences you take for granted. There were no smartphones, no internet, no instant access to information. When we faced challenges, we had to build the tools to solve them from scratch. Think about the microchip. In the 1950s, a couple of engineers, Jack Kilby and Robert Noyce, created something so small yet so powerful that it laid the foundation for every piece of technology you use today. Without that invention, your smartphone, your laptop, even the system that allows for global communication wouldn't exist." Eric crossed his arms, listening but not yet convinced.

"The internet," John continued, "which you and your friends use every day to connect with people all over the world, do you know how it started? It wasn't created in a vacuum. My generation, along with a lot of early Gen Xers, developed ARPANET in the 1960s. We didn't have a grand vision of social media or video streaming. We were just trying to create a way for computers to communicate across distances. Little by little, that project turned into the internet you rely on today." Eric sighed but didn't interrupt.

"And it's not just technology," John added. "Think about medicine. In the 1950s, Jonas Salk developed the polio vaccine. Do you realize how many children used to die or become paralyzed from that disease? Millions of lives were saved because of that vaccine. And it wasn't just polio—there were vaccines for measles, mumps, rubella. These were the advancements that allowed your generation to grow up healthy and safe from diseases that once ravaged entire communities." Eric shifted on his feet, the frustration in his eyes softening just a bit.

"I know things aren't perfect," John continued, his voice gentle but steady. "But my generation, and those before mine, weren't trying to destroy the world. We were solving the problems of our time, just like your generation is now trying to solve the problems of today. Yes, we relied on fossil fuels because that's what powered the world back then. Yes, we made decisions that had unintended consequences, but we also created the systems and infrastructure that allow you to live the life you do today." Eric slowly sat down on the porch step, looking out at the horizon, the orange glow of the setting sun reflecting in his eyes.

"You have to understand," John said, leaning back in his chair, "that each generation is part of a larger story. We didn't solve everything, but we gave you the tools to keep going. Your generation has done amazing things too. Look at how you've taken the internet and turned it into a tool for global connection, or how you've developed apps and platforms that make information accessible to anyone with a phone. And the advances in medicine, CRISPR, gene editing, artificial intelligence in diagnostics, those are all the work of Millennials and Gen Z. You've taken what we built and made it even better." Eric nodded slowly. "I get that... but it still feels like we're cleaning up a mess."

John smiled softly. "Every generation feels that way. My parents lived through the Great Depression and World War II. They thought they were cleaning up the mess left by the generation before them. And in many ways, they were. But they also built something in the process, something my generation was able to build on. And now, it's your turn. The problems you face may be different, but the solution isn't to tear down everything that came before. It's to take what works, fix what doesn't, and build something new." Eric looked up at his grandfather, understanding dawning in his eyes. "So… we're all part of this bigger picture?"

John nodded. "Exactly. We all contribute something, and it's not just about one generation being right or wrong. It's about recognizing that the world we live in today was shaped by every generation that came before. And it's up to your generation to shape what comes next." For the first time in the conversation, Eric smiled. "I guess I never thought about it like that."

John smiled back. "That's because sometimes we get so caught up in the problems, we forget to see the progress. Just remember, Eric, that each generation's contributions are vital. Together, we form the intricate, evolving fabric of human progress. What you do next will matter just as much as what we did." Eric nodded, his frustration replaced with a sense of purpose. He knew now that he wasn't just cleaning up the past—he was building the future.

The contrast between pre-Millennial and Millennial/Gen Z innovations highlights a shift in focus. Pre-Millennial generations were responsible for some of the most fundamental inventions that underpin modern society across the globe. Later generations have refined and repurposed these technologies, making them more accessible, interconnected, and user-friendly.

Older generations created the raw infrastructure like computers, the internet, vaccines, and transportation systems, while younger generations have specialized in scaling, optimizing, and democratizing these technologies. Millennials and Gen Z have focused more on application and enhancement, rather than fundamental, world-altering inventions. Yet they still demonize the older generations that made those innovations possible.

This contradiction highlights a deeper issue: younger generations are navigating a world of unprecedented convenience and access to information, yet they produce very little in the way of tangible contributions, and struggle with the complexities of creating meaningful change in systems that they both rely on and resist.

If Millennials and Gen Zers truly want to reshape society, they must grapple with the reality that meaningful progress requires both sacrifice and a willingness to rethink the comforts they have come to expect. Until then, their critiques will continue to ring hollow, drowned out by the buzzing of smartphones and the hum of cars on highways built by the very systems they condemn.

The mischaracterization of Boomers, Gen Jonesers, and early Gen Xers as enemies of progress is, at its core, a reflection of a deeper cultural shift. Millennials, Gen Y, and Gen Z have grown up in a world where personal success is often framed as an entitlement or right rather than something to be earned through perseverance and adaptability. This shift, combined with the cultural tendency to deflect responsibility, has led to a skewed understanding of the past and an unwillingness to acknowledge the contributions of older generations.

As a result, Boomers, Gen Jonesers, and early Gen Xers find themselves defending not just their personal achievements but the very systems they built to improve the lives of others.

They recognize that while the world is not perfect, it has improved in many ways because of their efforts. Their defensive posture is not born out of a refusal to change but out of a desire to ensure that the progress they fought for is not carelessly dismantled by those who fail to appreciate the struggles that came before them.

If younger generations can begin to see that their elders are not enemies but partners in the ongoing project of human progress, the generational divide may start to heal. Only by working together, with a shared sense of history and accountability, can society continue to move forward in a way that honors the past while building a better future.

If progress is to be truly sustainable, it will require a bridging of the generational divide. Younger generations must learn to appreciate the historical context in which their elders operated and recognize that the world they are eager to reshape was built through decades of hard work and struggle. Likewise, older generations must acknowledge that the world has changed and that younger people's calls for reform are born out of legitimate concerns.

Only by working together and learning from each other's experiences can society move forward in a way that honors the lessons of the past while embracing the opportunities of the future. The narrative that older generations are enemies of progress is not only oversimplified but dangerous, as it prevents meaningful dialogue and mutual understanding across the generations. Instead of focusing on blame, it is time to focus on solutions that incorporate the wisdom of the past with the energy and innovation of the future.

Bibliography

Abbate, Janet. Inventing the Internet. MIT Press, 1999.

Bellis, Mary. "The Invention of the Microchip." ThoughtCo., 2019. https://www.thoughtco.com/invention-of-the-microchip-1991411.

Brinkley, Alan. The Unfinished Nation: A Concise History of the American People. McGraw-Hill Education, 2013.

Grob, Gerald N., and Gerald Markowitz. The Politics of Vaccination: Practice and Policy in America's History. Routledge, 2005.

Isaacson, Walter. The Innovators: How a Group of Hackers, Geniuses, and Geeks Created the Digital Revolution. Simon & Schuster, 2014.

Kilby, Jack S. "Miniaturized Electronic Circuits." U.S. Patent No. 3,138,743. 23 June 1964.

Livingston, David. The Apollo Program: Missions to the Moon. National Aeronautics and Space Administration (NASA), 2004.

Mattick, John S., and Garvan Kanehisa. "Vaccines and Modern Medicine." New England Journal of Medicine, vol. 371, no. 10, 2014, pp. 928-937.

Salk, Jonas. Vaccines and the Fight Against Polio. University of Pittsburgh Press, 1957.

Waldrop, M. Mitchell. The Dream Machine: J.C.R. Licklider and the Revolution That Made Computing Personal. Penguin Books, 2001.

Zuboff, Shoshana. The Age of Surveillance Capitalism: The Fight for a Human Future at the New Frontier of Power. PublicAffairs, 2019.

This bibliography includes historical events, figures, and key inventions referenced in the conversation. Specific details from these sources are presented as part of a broader narrative, highlighting the role of pre-Millennial and Millennial generations in shaping modern society.